1 – Eugène Delacroix. *A Square in Seville* – 1832. Musée du Louvre, Cabinet des Dessins, Paris.

THE LANDSCAPE IN IMPRESSIONISM

The Impressionists were the painters of colour, light and atmosphere who initiated the adventure of modern art.

But when they showed their pictures for the first time, between 15 April and 15 May 1874, the public and the critics that came to see them in the studio of the photographer Nadar, Boulevard des Capucines, Paris, were far from enthusiastic. And it was one of the art critics who, after having seen Claude Monet's *Impression, Sunrise,* called them "Impressionists" for the first time.

The main protagonists of this new movement were all born between 1830 and 1841: Pissarro in 1830, Manet in 1832, Degas in 1834, Cézanne and Sisley in 1839, Monet in 1840, Renoir, Bazille, Guillaumin and Berthe Morisot in 1841. It was pure chance that they all met in Paris around 1860 and struck up stimulating friendships. They came from two separate groups: Pissarro and Cézanne from the Académie Charles Suisse; Monet, Renoir, Sisley and Bazille from the Gleyre studio. And thus the two main trends of Impressionism were already visible: the Pontoise trend, pastoral and terrestrial,

2 – Eugène Delacroix.
*Sketch-Book from Morocco –
1832 (pages 23 v° and 24 r°).*
Musée du Louvre,
Cabinet des Dessins, Paris.

3 – Anton van Dyck. *Landscape
with a Harbour in the
Background.* Barber Institute
of Fine Arts, Birmingham.

THE LANDSCAPE
IN
IMPRESSIONISM

PARK
LANE

true to Corot's legacy, and the Argenteuil trend which tried to convey the mobility of water and the variations of light. Although they had different origins, temperaments and culture, they were all driven by a common aspiration: they longed to free themselves from official culture so as to paint sincerely. And in addition to revolutionizing painting formally they also assumed a new manner and a new attitude towards modern life, depicting it with joyful exaltation. They observed the multiple aspects of nature – the silence of the forests, the majesty of the seascapes, the luminosity of the regatta, the green of the countryside, the bustle on the Seine river. Their enormous creative strength was mocked and scorned by their contemporaries, public and critics, who were fond of historical subjects, religious or classical scenes, portraits and, last of all, traditional landscapes, still considered as a minor form of art. Traditional culture and genre painting were omnipotent: a member of the Ecole des Beaux-Arts since 1825, Ingres had succeeded David at the Académie des Beaux-Arts where he taught the supremacy of line over colour and looked down on Corot's landscapes and Delacroix's compositions as "badly drawn" for lack of a clear contour line around the subjects.

The young painters with an independent mind who refused to attend the traditional Académie studied with Charles Suisse or Charles Gleyre and copied the Louvre paintings. In the evening they met in the cafés where they spent hours talking about painting and debating on the respective qualities of Ingres and his superiority of line and Delacroix and his supremacy of colour. The latter's influence could still be felt quite strongly. A man of his times, Delacroix (1798-1863) painted historical themes which – like the members of the Académie – he still considered the noblest subject. He was, however, to show the way to the Impressionists with his small landscapes full of coloured structures which make him the direct precursor of the realism of light. In 1832 Delacroix travelled to Spain and Morocco and was deeply impressed by this short experience from which he derived so many suggestions and subjects. He brought back a few small landscapes (*A Square in Seville*, 1832, plate 1) painted in watercolours, the straightforward technique launched by the English

4 – François-Marius Granet. *The Seine Riverside in the Fog* – 1843. Musée du Louvre, Cabinet des Dessins, Paris.

5 – John Constable. *Wivenhoe Park* (detail) – 1816. National Gallery of Art, Washington, D.C.

6 – Johann Christian Dahl. *Cloud Study* – Art Gallery, Göteborg.

7 – John Constable. *Near Stoke-by-Nayland* – 1807 ca. The Tate Gallery, London.

painters, where the colour range of the greenery brings to mind the Impressionists and also the watercolour studies painted by Cézanne towards the end of his life in the countryside around Aix.

A pupil of David's and a friend of Ingres's, François-Marius Granet (1775-1849) painted landscapes in scenes of the classic antiquity, with real or fantastic ruins and also some watercolours that reveal his keen sensitivity to the impact of light on objects, thus making him a forerunner of Impressionism. His picture *The Seine Riverside in the Fog* (1843, plate 4) clearly shows that the painter entirely neglects the drawing and uses his brush to convey his feelings about the scenery lost in the fog.

Landscape Painting in the Nineteenth Century

Landscape painting was discovered again in the Romantic era and produced its best results in England. English painting became known in France between 1820 and 1830, when relations with England were resumed after the Revolution and the Empire. It was in this period that various travel books were published in France that divulgated simple and immediate regional topographic views. It was the first time that the general public got acquainted with a number of French places depicted in such a way: the coasts of the Channel or the Seine river area in which so many landscape painters were later to become interested. The French artists were highly interested in English landscape, and an exhibition of their pictures held in Paris at the 1824 Salon met with an immense success. It was then that Constable was awarded a gold medal and Delacroix defined him as "the father of our landscape painting." Its main exponent was John Constable (1776-1837), the bard of clouds and skies, luxuriant countryside, green pastures and wind-swept silence (*Near Stoke-by-Nayland*, 1807 ca., plate 7; *Wivenhoe Park*, detail, 1816, plate 5).

7

Anton van Dick (1599-1641) was one of the forerunners of the English watercolourists. During a journey in England he felt a sudden interest in the representation of nature (*Landscape with a Harbour in the Background*, plate 3, undoubtedly his best landscape drawing).

Among the numerous painters that depicted landscapes and the various aspects of nature, we must also mention Johann Christian Dahl (1788-1857), considered the main Scandinavian landscape painter (*Cloud Study*, plate 6).

The Barbizon School

The Impressionists' direct forerunners were the painters of the Barbizon School (also called the 1830 School or Fontainebleau School).

The term is generally used to qualify a group of artists – among which were Théodore Rousseau, Jean-François Millet, Jules Dupré, Constant Troyon, Virgile-Narcisse Diaz de la Peña, Charles-François Daubigny, Alexandre-Gabriel Decamps, Charles-Emile Jacque, Georges Michel and minor landscape or animal painters such as Brascassat or Rosa Bonheur – that met around the elder ones; as the fame of the School increased during the second half of the century, the group became more and more numerous.

By the time Rousseau became famous, Camille Corot (1796-1875) had already painted a number of masterpieces. He may be considered an exponent of that School because of the characteristics of his composition, his choice of subjects and a kind of evocatory inspiration in some of his paintings. He had devoted himself to painting in 1822 and – following the classical canons – practised directly from nature in the Fontainebleau forest and along the Channel coast. In winter he would paint for the Salon in his studio: large-size works true to the tradition of Lorrain or Poussin, and in summer he would travel about France and paint in the open. It was during his many visits to Fontainebleau that he met Rousseau, Troyon, Diaz and Dupré. He became a great friend of Daubigny, and he took him to the Morvan region (*Cornfield in Morvan*, 1842, plate 15; *The Marissel Church*, 1866, plate 21).

At the beginning of the nineteenth century some small farmers had settled on the edge of the Fontainebleau forest some seventy kilometers from Paris, where the Brie plain starts, and had built small villages. One of these villages, Barbizon, was to give its name to the artistic counter-culture of which Théodore Rousseau is considered the founder.

The first painters settled there in July 1830. They had grown tired of city life and were attracted by the beauty and genuineness of this part of nature. They lodged in farmhouses or at the village inn, and at the crack of dawn, when the village started moving, they went to paint in the Bas-Bréau glade, the thick forest of Gros-Foutu or the Apremont gorge near Mareaux-Fées, staying there till sunset. They had the com-

8 – Théodore Rousseau. *A Tree in the Fontainebleau Forest* – 1840.
Victoria and Albert Museum, London.

mon aim of faithfully observing nature but each of them followed his own character.

In the open they sketched various sections and later on in their studios they painted the whole picture or, like Corot, in order to retain a unity of tone, they used the same sky-trees-ground ensemble for each sitting and finished their pictures in their studios. In August 1849 a new railway line enabled Parisians to get to Fontainebleau in an hour and a half, whereas eight hours had been necessary for the same journey by coach. Fontainebleau then became one of the favourite places for country outings, and landscape painters flocked there in ever larger numbers.

9 – Théodore Rousseau. *Landscape.* Municipal Museum, De Nittis Gallery, Barletta.

10 – Georges Michel. *Landscape* – 1835.
Stedelijk Museum, Amsterdam.

"To hell with civilization, hurray for nature and poetry," was the battle-cry of Rousseau (1812-1867). He was the first to patronize Barbizon in 1836 and was followed by Diaz, Millet, Jacque, Corot and Daubigny. His culture – marked by eighteenth-century rationalism – and his analytical mind induced him to try to be as precise as possible and represent every single detail of reality, to re-create the natural world on his canvas as if it were a living organism. Between 1826 and 1829 he painted pictures directly from nature in the countryside around Paris, and also copied the Dutch landscape painters of the seventeenth-century. Like many artists in his circles, he was a democrat at heart and was deeply disap-

11 – Jules Dupré. *The Lock* – 1846 ca. Musée du Louvre, Paris.

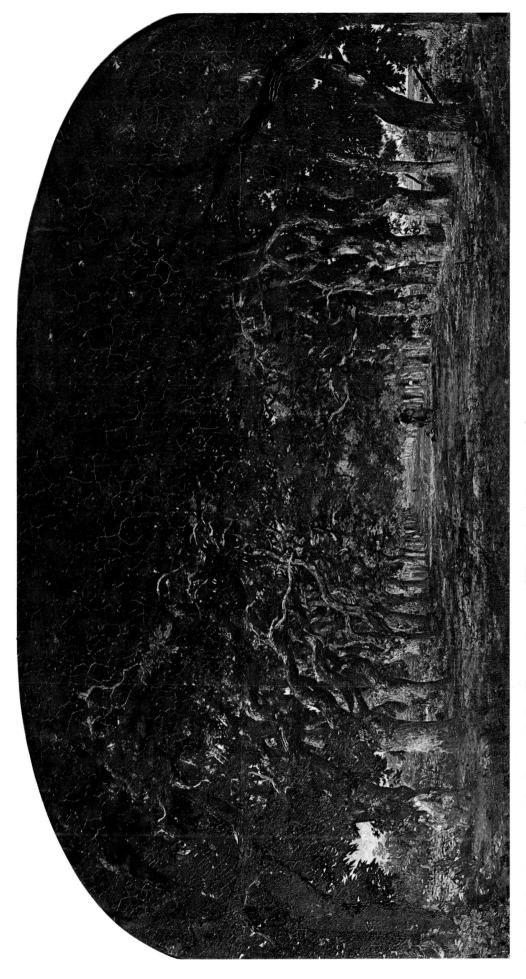

12 – Théodore Rousseau. *The Lane with the Chestnut Trees* – 1837. Musée du Louvre, Paris.

13 – Constant Troyon. *Landscape near Paris* – 1849.
Museum of Fine Arts, Henry C. and Martha B.
Angeli Collection, Boston.

pointed by the outcome of the 1830 riots, when Louis-Phi-
lippe d'Orléans ascended the throne and became the king of
the French. He felt that the dream of simplicity and purity
which had been the idealistic yearning of the bourgeoisie
could only be realised through direct contact with nature and
isolation in the woods.

In 1834 he started travelling a lot, giving his preference to
the most primitive and wildest regions, such as the Jura, the
Fontainebleau forest (*A Tree in the Fontainebleau Forest*,
1840, plate 8) or the Vendée (*The Lane with the Chestnut
Trees*, 1837, plate 12). After 1840 he followed the advice of
his friend Dupré and chose a more peaceful and uniform type
of landscape. In 1844, with Dupré, he stayed in the Landes
and in Berry and devoted all his efforts to the direct study of
nature, especially to light and atmospheric effects. In 1849
he settled for good at Barbizon and struck up a deep friendship with Millet. There, he bent his sensitivity to the objective
study of nature, increasingly working directly from nature
and concentrating on rendering the light effects at certain
moments of the day as well as the luminosity of the atmosphere (*A Road in the Fontainebleau Forest*, 1860-65, plate
17; *The Cart*, 1862, plate 14).

14 – Théodore Rousseau. *The Cart* – 1862.
Musée du Louvre, Paris.

Jules Dupré (1811-1889) was Rousseau's friend. He had made his first appearance at the 1831 Salon with three landscapes and was immediately appreciated and hailed as one of the greatest exponents of Romantic landscape painting. Few paintings have remained from the period of his friendship with Rousseau. The most famous, *The Lock* (1846 ca., plate 11), summarizes the melancholy aspect of the landscape. He grew less and less interested in the direct study of nature and conceived landscapes according to his own mental schemes and sentimental dispositions, all of which explain the Romantic characteristics of his works (*Sunset on the Marsh*, 1855-60, plate 18).

Constant Troyon (1810-1865) is one of the numerous painters who frequented Barbizon. Like Dupré or Diaz he had started as a ceramics painter. He was awarded a first-class medal for his pictures (*Landscape near Paris*, 1849, plate 13) which appealed to both art critics and the general public.

We must also mention Georges Michel (1763-1843) whose wide landscapes are characterized by leaden tempestuous skies which appealed to the young Rousseau (*Landscape*, 1835, plate 10).

However, the only real heir to Rousseau's ideas and sensitiv-

15 – Jean-Baptiste-Camille Corot. *Cornfield in Morvan* – 1842. Musée des Beaux-Arts, Lyon.

16 – Charles-François Daubigny. *Beach*. Stedelijk Museum, Amsterdam.

17 – Théodore Rousseau. *A Road in the Fontainebleau Forest* – 1860-65. Musée du Louvre, Paris.

18 – Jules Dupré. *Sunset on the Marsh* – 1855-60. Musée du Louvre, Paris.

19 – Jean-François Millet. *Spring* – 1868-73. Musée du Louvre, Paris.

ity was Jean-François Millet (1814-1875) who started painting his typical and artistically more mature works after the
1848 Revolution. He was born in Normandy in 1837 and was
able to settle in Paris to study more thoroughly thanks to a
grant which Cherbourg, his native town, had awarded him. "I
am a peasant and nothing but a peasant," he declared when
he was confronted with Paris, that "gloomy, chaotic town."
In 1849 he settled at Barbizon with his large family and, apart
from brief spells, was to spend the rest of his life there.
Together with Rousseau he became the nucleus of a small
community – the reference point for all the "Barbizonniers" –
founded on solidarity, friendship and common plans for their

future works. In order to convey his message and moral
ideal – born from his opposition to the modern industrial-
ized world – he went on painting peasants at work in their
fields. His pessimism is even more evident in the works of
his last period: the hostile earth resists, indifferent to man's
fatigue.
"In the country I can find infinite splendours ... tragedy is
surrounded with splendour." Flowers, emerald seascapes,

20 – Charles-François Daubigny. *Landscape* – 1877.
The Metropolitan Museum of Art, New York.

21

21 – Jean-Baptiste-Camille Corot. *The Marissel Church* – 1866. Musée du Louvre, Paris.

spring fields (*Spring*, 1868-73, plate 19) are the splendour; the tragedy is man's desperate toil and trouble.

Charles-François Daubigny (1817-1878) is a key figure between Romantic sensitivity and Impressionism. He was born in Paris and spent his whole life there, devoting himself to graphics and book and magazine illustrations, keeping his landscape painting in the background. Like a true townsman,

he often escaped to the country and explored many parts of France. In 1836 he travelled to Italy, a six months' journey, the dream of his youth. In 1842 Fontainebleau disappointed him because of the climate and the insects. In 1842, in Morvan, he met Corot who gave him a greater interest in natural landscapes.

The Morvan region was an ideal place for him: "a picturesque area, waterfalls, woods, mountains, slopes ... all of them surprisingly wild." And the public quite liked his landscapes which he reduced to well-known schemes.

His friendship with Corot – a pleasant friend and good ad-

22 – Gustave Courbet. *Beach*. National Museum, Warsaw.

23 – Gustave Courbet. *The Etretat Cliff after a Storm* – 1869. Musée d'Orsay, Paris.

viser – was precious for Daubigny who paid much attention to the changing and fugitive aspects of the landscape (*Beach*, plate 16; *Landscape*, 1877, plate 20) which he painted from nature as he sailed his boat "le Botin" in the suburbs of Paris, in the Isère region or along the Channel coasts.

In the years which immediately preceded the impressionist period, Daubigny met with the same type of opposition from the art critics. Gautier wrote in 1861: "What a pity that an authentic landscape painter, so just and natural, should be satisfied with an impression and so evidently neglect the details."

The Beaches of the North

Before settling for good on the banks of the Seine and Oise rivers, Monet and his companions hesitated between the trees and rocks of the Fontainebleau forest and the Channel beaches which the English watercolourists liked so much at the beginning of the century.

Thanks to the new fashion for sea-bathing imported from England, all along the coast from Honfleur to Cabourg, the small fishermen's villages had become elegant seaside resorts frequented by intellectuals and the upper bourgeoisie who could now reach them easily by train. The tourist guides

24

24 – Johan Barthold Jongkind. *Harbour in the Evening* – Rijksmuseum Kröller-Müller, Otterlo.

of the time recommended taking a trip up the Seine, on the ship that daily linked Rouen and Le Havre.

During the Barbizon period Normandy went out of fashion but, between 1858 and 1870, it became a centre for open air painting. This was largely due to Eugène Boudin (1824-1898) who was born and lived all his life in Honfleur – with the exception of a short spell in Paris.

The suggestive aspects of his native coast, the variegated hues of the sky reflected on the sea according to the time and season and the liveliness of the beaches peopled by bathers were his favourite themes (*The Bordeaux Harbour*, 1874, plate 25; *Empress Eugénie on the Trouville Beach*, 1863, plate 26).

He was a gracious host for Johan Barthold Jongkind (1819-1891), a Dutch painter who spent his restless anguished life between Paris and the coasts of Normandy and Provence. He kept seeking in nature a correspondence for his inner restlessness, and his painting reflects his fantasy and nervous immediacy (*Harbour in the Evening*, plate 24).

It was thanks to Boudin that in 1859, Gustave Courbet (1818-1877), the most authoritative spokesman of Realism, discovered Le Havre and the sea and painted his first seascapes. He was to come back to those beaches every summer: in 1866 at Deauville, to which he invited Monet and Jongkind; in 1867 at Saint-Aubin-sur-Mer, in Calvados; at Le Havre in 1868 and 1869.

25 – Eugène Boudin. *The Bordeaux Harbour* – 1874. National Gallery, Edinburgh.

26 – Eugène Boudin. *Empress Eugénie on the Trouville Beach* – 1863. Art Gallery, Glasgow.

At Etretat, where marvellous cliffs tower above the beach, he painted a whole series of calm or stormy seascapes, where the greens, browns and greys are as natural as the rocks, trees, sea and sky (*Beach*, plate 22; *The Etretat Cliff after a Storm*, 1869, plate 23).

It was Monet (1840-1926) who introduced his friends to the beaches of the North for he had lived at Le Havre where he drew caricatures. Then Boudin had convinced him to go to Paris in order to take some drawing and painting lessons. In 1862, after serving in Algeria, he came back to Le Havre where he renewed his friendship with Boudin and met Jongkind.

The two artists became friends and travelled together, painting the countryside around Sainte-Adresse and numerous seascapes.

In 1863 he settled in Paris to study more thoroughly and, in summer, after the lessons at the Gleyre studio, the group of friends took the train from Paris and went to paint after nature in the Fontainebleau forest. They got off at Avon or Melun and went on foot to Chailly-en-Bière, like Monet or Bazille, or to Marlotte, Renoir and Sisley's favourite spot.

The Fontainebleau experience left a deep mark on the lives of all the Impressionists who kept pursuing their ideal of representing landscapes and nature and never lost their love for the countryside.

In 1864 Monet accompanied Frédéric Bazille to Normandy. Both men sailed down the Seine, thronging with the steamboats, tugs and barges that sailed up and down between Paris and Le Havre.

The following year Renoir and Sisley also went down the Seine on a sailboat from Paris to Le Havre, and Degas himself, par excellence painter of town life who never worked in the open, went to Boulogne-sur-Mer in 1869 with Monet.

There he looked at the dunes and beaches, drawing quick sketches of the scenery that Boudin loved so dearly, conveying with great delicacy their damp atmosphere and iridescent light. A few quick strokes sufficed to suggest, in the distance, the presence of boats or men (*By the Seaside*, 1869 ca., plate 40).

The Seine River

Whereas the beaches of Normandy were a fashionable refuge for the rich, on Sundays and feast days the Parisians flocked to the small riverside inns in the suburbs of Paris and devoted themselves to the pleasures of rowing, which was quite fashionable at the time, and dancing in the suburban café-restaurants. The painters mingled with the happy common people and repeatedly depicted rowers, pretty young women, parties on the grass and regattas.

27 – Pierre-Auguste Renoir. *The Champs-Elysées during the 1867 Universal Exhibition.* Private collection.

28 – Pierre-Auguste Renoir. *La Grenouillère* – 1869. Nationalmuseum, Stockholm.

29 – Claude Monet. *La Grenouillère* – 1869. The Metropolitan Museum of Art, Havenmeyer Collection, New York.

30 – Camille Pissarro. *February, Dawn, Bazincourt* – 1893. Rijksmuseum Kröller-Müller, Otterlo.

31 – Camille Pissarro. *The Gisors-Pontoise Road, Snow Effect* – 1873. Museum of Fine Arts, Boston.

32 – Alfred Sisley. *Banks of the Seine at Bougival* (detail) – 1867. Private collection.

33 – Claude Monet. *Regatta at Argenteuil, Grey Weather* – 1874. Musée du Louvre, Paris.

34 – Pierre-Auguste Renoir. *The Seine at Argenteuil* – 1873-74. Portland Art Museum Collection, Portland (Oregon).

35 – Camille Pissarro. *Orchard at Louveciennes* – 1870-72 ca. Private collection.

In 1869 **Monet** was living at Bougival where he had been able to rent a house with the help of Gaudibert, the art dealer. Above all a painter of the water, Monet was charmed by the Seine, its reflections, its plays of light and its transparencies; with his friend Renoir he was a regular visitor to that stretch of river, dotted with islets and frequented by a motley crowd. Side by side they painted the famous landing stage of *La Grenouillère*, where row boats thronged. Without any hesita-tion or retouching they faithfully depicted the constant dia-logue between light and water, and each of them expressed his own reality, according to his feelings. Renoir's *La Gre-nouillère* (1869, plate 28), full of light and harmonious col-ours, is represented as a scenario of human figures, in which the artist captures the details of the clothes. In Monet's picture (*La Grenouillère*, 1869, plate 29), there are fewer boats and figures. Since he wishes to give a more complete

36 – Camille Pissarro. *View of the Seine River from the Pont Neuf* – 1901. Staechelin Collection, Basel.

representation of the subject, Monet puts the surface of the river in the foreground and highlights the vibrations of the light effects on the water. These two pictures mark the birth of impressionist painting and clearly reveal the difference between Monet, an endless inventor of techniques and types of vision, and Renoir, always open to any theme, who warms everything he paints with human kindness: familiar images of everyday life on the Seine, in the fields and on the streets of Paris and the joyous balls of the Moulin de la Galette (*The Champs-Elysées during the 1867 Universal Exhibition*, plate 27).

Pierre-Auguste Renoir (1841-1919) had started working as a porcelain painter and had then switched over to the more lucrative task of painting fans and material.

In 1862 he attended the lessons at the Gleyre studio and, with his friends, frequented the Café Guerbois, Rue des Batignol-

37 – Camille Pissarro. *The Red Roofs,*
View of a Village in Winter –
1887. Musée d'Orsay, Paris.

38 – Alfred Sisley. *The Flood at Port-Marly* (detail) – 1876. Musée d'Orsay, Paris.

39 – Camille Pissarro. *Hermitage at Pontoise* (detail) – 1878. Kunstmuseum, Basel.

40 – Edgar Degas. *By the Seaside* – 1869 ca. Musée du Louvre, Cabinet des Dessins, Paris.

les. They were united by their common love for painting, their lack of money and the desire to be acknowledged and appreciated.

This café was also patronized by Nadar, the photographer, a few art critics and famous writers such as Zola, a childhood friend of Paul Cézanne's.

Together they decided to set up an exhibition, but the 1870 Franco-Prussian war and economical problems obliged them to postpone it. It was not held until 1874 in Nadar's studio.

The war caused the Impressionists to split up: Frédéric Bazille, Monet's generous friend who had so often helped him financially, had enlisted and was to die shortly. To avoid fighting Monet had left for England, like Pissarro whom he was to meet again in London; together they met with Paul Durand-Ruel, who had also sought refuge in Great Britain and was later to become the Impressionists' dealer in Paris.

Anonymous and miserable refugees, Monet and Pissarro visited the museums and painted in the open air in the foggy atmosphere of the Thames, a theme which Monet was to repeat in 1904 when he came back to London and painted a famous series of 37 pictures (*Parliament, London: Sunlight in the Fog*, 1904, plate 44).

When the war and the Commune came to an end, Monet travelled back to France via Holland, where he was especially attracted by Zaandam, a picturesque place on the Zaan river. While his wife gave French lessons, he painted this flat countryside with rare vigour (*Windmill near Zaandam*, 1871, plate 41).

Back in France he settled at Argenteuil and, for a few years, that village on the banks of the Seine was to become one of the centres of Impressionism.

The Argenteuil School

In those days Argenteuil offered a unique impression, with the Seine widening into a lake where boatmen went rowing and fields that stretched as far as the eye could see. Monet had an old boat with a rudimentary cabin which he used to host his friends and to paint on the water.

When the boatmen organized races, the painter was on site to capture the hovering sails onto his canvas, attracted by the

41 – Claude Monet. *Windmill near Zaandam* – 1871. Private collection.

42 – Claude Monet. *Fishermen in a Boat near Zaandam* – 1883. Private collection.

43 – Claude Monet. *The Poppies near Argenteuil* – 1875. Private collection.

44 – Claude Monet. *Parliament, London: Sunlight in the Fog* – 1904. Musée du Louvre, Paris.

45 – Paul Cézanne. *Zola's House at Médan* – 1880 ca. Art Gallery and Museum, Burrel Collection, Glasgow.

silver-green colour of the river (*Regatta at Argenteuil, Grey Weather*, 1874, plate 33).

During the summer of 1873 and in 1874, he was joined by Renoir who was also charmed by the sight of the boats and boatmen which he depicted alongside of Monet. In his picture *The Seine at Argenteuil* (1873-74, plate 34), he focuses on the figures, drawing close to the subject as he had done for *La Grenouillère* (plate 28).

Like Monet, Renoir depicted the countryside around Argenteuil, but the former used a new vibrating and colourful technique to render the drunken sensations of one who, accustomed to living in a city, immerses himself freely in the fields (*The Poppies near Argenteuil*, 1875, plate 43).

Sisley, who lived at Port-Marly, near Bougival, also visited Monet. Born in France of English parents, Sisley (1839-1889) had not been called up during the war and had settled

46 – Paul Cézanne. *The Maincy Bridge* (detail) – 1882-85. Musée du Louvre, Paris.

47 – Paul Cézanne. *Village Seen through the Trees* – 1885 ca. Kunsthalle, Bremen.

near the Seine river. Up to that moment the money which his parents sent him had spared him the task of working for a living.

But the war brought about his father's bankruptcy and he had to devote himself entirely to painting to support his wife and children.

Although he maintained his independence, he was one of the first to participate in the impressionist movement. He was solely a landscape painter and painted exclusively the Ile-de-France region (*Banks of the Seine*, 1876, plate 32). A painter of water, he was also attracted by the frequent floods of the Seine and, in 1872, he inquired into the effects of the flood in the Ile-de-la-Loi and on the road from Saint-Germain to Port-Marly.

In 1876, as he had only a short distance to go, he repeatedly reproduced on his canvas the floods at Port-Marly.

Despite the tragic theme and a heavy sky foreboding fresh rain, his pictures are bathed in a sort of serene peace. He succeeds in capturing the coming of spring in the buds of the still bare trees while the cream and pink tones of the Nicolas house convey a sense of calm (*The Flood at Port-Marly*, 1876, plate 38).

The Pontoise School

Pontoise is the principal town of the Vexin, a fertile area between Normandy and the Seine river. It is one of the places where the Impressionists lived in their constant quest for better living and working conditions. The most prominent figure of this quiet part of France was Pissarro who lived and worked there for more than thirty years. In his eyes the Vexin embodied the calm and solidity of the country, with its houses strewn about the gently sloping hills and the regular succes-

49

49 – Paul Cézanne. *Mount Sainte-Victoire* (detail) – 1904-06 ca. Philadelphia Museum of Art.

sion of the seasons and days, a world that could not but appeal to one who loved the country so intensely.

He was born in the West Indies, in the French colony of Saint-Thomas, and settled in Paris in 1855, just in time to see the English landscape painters at the "Expo" and meet Courbet at the Pavillon du Réalisme. In Paris he first attended the Ecole des Beaux-Arts and then the Académie Suisse where he met Cézanne and the other Impressionists, but he preferred painting in the suburbs of Paris. His two favourite themes

48 – Paul Cézanne. *In the Black Castle Park* (detail) – 1900 ca. Musée du Louvre, Paris.

were the houses perched on the hills and the roads seen in perspective.

In 1864 he settled at Osny, a village near Pontoise, bringing with him two painters who were to become famous in time, Cézanne and Gauguin. His wanderings through the winding streets of Pontoise or in the neighbourhood soon became familiar; just a few steps and he could roam about the orchards, the fields and the country paths that led into the very heart of the chestnut and hazelnut woods that surrounded the village.

In 1869 he left Pontoise for three years and settled first at Louveciennes (*Orchard at Louveciennes*, 1870-72 ca., plate 35)

51

50 – Paul Gauguin. *Towards the Village* – 1879. Museum of Fine Arts, Boston.

and then in London with Claude Monet, during the Franco-Prussian war, to avoid fighting. It was in London that he discovered the English painters' watercolours and learnt to see "the light."

He went back to Pontoise in 1872 and went on painting the same subjects: patches of greenery and trees, but with a lighter palette (*The Gisors-Pontoise Road, Snow Effect*, 1873, plate 31; *Hermitage at Pontoise*, 1878, plate 39; *The Red Roofs, View of a Village in Winter*, 1887, plate 37).

Broad-minded and always open to the others, he shared Seurat's and Signac's pointillistic experiment between 1885 and 1890 and took part in the first Divisionist exhibition in 1886; four years later he left this intellectual trend to return to a "less scientific" painting. It was at that time that the river, a favourite theme of the Argenteuil Impressionists, appeared in his painting (*February, Dawn, Bazincourt*, 1893, plate 30). His long life – he was to die in 1903 – allowed him to reap the fruits of his labour and he was able to divide his time between Paris, his family, journeys to England and Belgium, and very frequent trips to Normandy.

Paul Cézanne was born in 1839 at Aix-en-Provence into a wealthy middle-class family. Quite early his father had to accept Paul's decision to devote himself to arts and allowed him to settle in Paris where he attended lessons at the Académie Suisse and became friends with Pissarro the only painter whose temperament he felt close to. He alternated

51 – Paul Gauguin. *Landscape at Le Pouldu* – 1890. National Gallery of Art, Washington, D.C.

staying in Paris and retiring to Aix, where he finally settled after his father's death. At the beginning of 1872 he moved to Pontoise and then to Auvers, to the home of Doctor Gachet, an art lover who was to be van Gogh's host before the latter's death.

When he was in Paris, he lived in a tiny flat with his model and mistress, Hortense Fiquet; he lived in poverty and even concealed his son Paul's birth. It was his friend Pissarro who advised him to go and live in the country, where rents were lower and where he could paint in the open. And thus the two groups, those that had existed in Paris in 1860, corresponding to the two basic trends of Impressionism but with the same interest in sincerity and the same spirit of brotherly com-

petition, reformed: the Argenteuil group around Monet and the Pontoise group around Pissarro.

The Vexin countryside and light were quite different from those that Cézanne had liked in Provence, but Pissarro's example transformed his palette: he eliminated dark colours, apart from black which became lighter, while he grew more sensitive to light effects and changing tones. Cézanne experienced financial difficulties since the allowance which his father sent him was not up to his needs and since both the 1874 exhibition, and the 1876 exhibition had been failures. Then, during the third exhibition in 1877, the critics began to take an interest in him. It was then that Cézanne's indifference to all that was not painting induced him to retire. This

53 – Paul Gauguin. *The Blue Roof* (*Farmyard at Le Pouldu*) – 1890. Private collection.

period of isolation best suited his solitary temper for he desired no publicity around his name. And so he returned to Provence, with its dark austere beauty, and gave vent to his craving for an architecture of forms, which he built according to rigid geometrical structures. It was then that he elaborated his so-called "constructive period" (*Village Seen through the Trees*, 1885 ca., plate 47), which certain non-impressionistic elements in his Pontoise and Auvers works had already heralded (*Zola's House at Médan*, 1880 ca., plate 45).
His mature period culminates in the pictures he painted at the

52 – Paul Gauguin. *Huts under the Trees* (*Martinique*) – 1887. Private collection.

Jas de Bouffan, the big country estate which his father had left him and where he found the ideal surroundings for his life and work. He would paint in the harsh Provence sunlight and was especially attracted by Mount Sainte-Victoire which rose above the plain behind Garenne. Sometimes he depicted it as a low and bulky mountain, sometimes as a high and steep mass looming above the valley or towering above a vast plain framed by pine-trees in the distance (*Mount Sainte-Victoire*, 1904-06 ca., plate 49). During the last ten years of his life, his search for luminosity and transparency induced him to give growing importance to watercolours, no longer as mere sketches but as truly complete works like his most finished paintings.

55

55 – Vincent van Gogh. *Thatched Cottages at Cordeville* – 1890. Musée du Louvre, Paris.

Neo-Impressionism

In 1876 Paul Gauguin met Pissarro at his tutor's. At the time he was a moderately gifted amateur painter. After leaving the navy in 1871, he had found a job at a stockbroker's and his life followed the traditional rhythm of the bourgeois way of life: he had married a rich Danish woman, had some children and made money at the stock exchange. During his leisure time he painted with his colleague Emile Schuffenecker. Camille Pissarro introduced him to the impressionist group

54 – Vincent van Gogh. *The Café Terrace on the Place du Forum, Arles, at Night* – September 1888. Rijksmuseum Kröller-Müller, Otterlo.

and he became friends with Paul Cézanne with whom he painted around Pontoise, where he was attracted by the countryside (*Towards the Village*, 1879, plate 50).

Neither Monet nor Renoir liked his painting and, as a sign of protest, they both refused to participate in the fifth impressionist exhibition in 1880 where Gauguin publicly showed his works for the first time, patronized by Pissarro. "The dauber," as Monet called him, had in any case decided to devote all his time to painting and, in 1873, after a vain attempt at reconciling work and painting, he left his well-paid job at the stock exchange and his family.

In spite of his miserable life – he was reduced to bill sticking – and notwithstanding his illness, he relentlessly devoted

57

56 – Vincent van Gogh. *The Langlois Bridge, Arles* – 1888. Wallraf-Richartz Museum, Cologne.

himself to painting and experimented in a new direction, with respect to the period when he studied Cézanne, to derive a new impulse and a less empirical construction of the latter's works.

In order to lead a simpler life he left Paris and settled in Brittany, at Pont-Aven, where life was cheaper. The artists knew that at Madame Gloannec's inn they could delay payment for their room and board.

The pictures he painted at Pont-Aven in the summer of 1887 and those he painted in Panama and Martinique when he fled from civilization for the first time show a greater rigour in

the composition and a greater exuberance in the warm high-keyed colours (*Huts under the Trees (Martinique)*, 1887, plate 52). Henceforth Gauguin was to give the human figure a significant presence and use it to give life to the places he depicted.

When he came back to Pont-Aven in 1888, he had reached his full maturity, and the pictures he was to paint until 1891 asserted an arbitrary anti-naturalistic colour, directly inspired by his emotions (*The Blue Roof (Farmyard at Le Pouldu)*, 1890, plate 53). His moment of glory had come; numerous painters followed him in Brittany and considered him as the

57 – Vincent van Gogh. *Boats on the Beach at the Saintes-Maries* (detail) – 1888. Rijksmuseum Vincent van Gogh, Amsterdam.

prophet of a new language. And whereas his 1888 and 1889 exhibitions were financial failures, they were nevertheless a stimulating revelation for the painters who dreamt of a direct form of art, which could capture an emotional and symbolic truth beyond the appearances of reality.

But Gauguin had decided to run away from civilization and search for a primitive way of life. He settled in Tahiti from 1891 to 1893 and, after a short stay in Paris, he went back there in 1895. He led a miserable and solitary life until 1901, when he left for the Dominican island of Marquesas where he died in 1903 at the age of 65.

Gauguin had met Vincent van Gogh in Paris in 1886. Théo van Gogh, the latter's brother who managed the Montmartre branch of the Galerie Goupil, had introduced the two artists to each other.

Vincent van Gogh was born in 1853 at Zundert in Holland into a family where Protestant ministers had alternated with art dealers, and for many years Vincent was torn between painting and mysticism. He sold pictures in his uncles' gallery in the Hague and then decided to study for admittance to the seminary.

Having miserably failed his examinations, he devoted him-

59 – Vincent van Gogh. *Crows in the Wheatfields, Auvers* (detail) – 1890. Rijksmuseum Vincent van Gogh, Amsterdam.

self to lay preaching in the Borinage, where he shared the miners' miserable lives. In 1886 he joined his brother in Paris. Théo was to help him and be his confidant for the rest of his life. It was thanks to Théo that he met the Impressionists. He was especially charmed by Gauguin's personality and by the power of his pictorial works. Van Gogh was an apostle at heart and needed to communicate his ideas and compare them with those of other people. He dreamed of constituting a new family of artists with diverse personalities.

No one knows exactly why, in 1888, he left Paris for Provence, where he dreamed of creating "the friends' house." He arrived at Arles in February and, with Théo's help, rented a flat. There he painted in the open, dazzled by the light, attracted by the vast plain of the Crau, the cypresses and olive trees.

He relentlessly painted more than 200 pictures which he piled up in his studio, the surface of the canvas taken up by the minute description of the various elements he sees, which he is always careful to link together with roads, paths or alleys.

58 – Vincent van Gogh. *The Cypresses* – 1889.
    The Metropolitan Museum of Art,
    Rogers Fund 1949, New York.

That is the reason why bridges are so important: they constitute the central part of many of his paintings (*The Langlois Bridge, Arles*, 1888, plate 56).

At the beginning of June he went on a pilgrimage to the Saintes-Maries-de-la-Mer where he discovered an unexpectedly violet sea (*Boats on the Beach at the Saintes-Maries*, 1888, plate 57).

He got back to Arles at the height of summer and spent all his time painting in the fields in the hot sunshine. He used the most violent colours, knowing that "time will tone them down even too much." Yellow is the colour that distinguishes the Arles period from others (*The Café Terrace on the Place du Forum, Arles, at Night*, September 1888, plate 54).

In September Gauguin came and lived with him. After the first moments of work in common, the two painters, so different in personality, started quarrelling violently and finally had a furious fight on Christmas Eve. When Gauguin decided to leave Arles, van Gogh cut off his left ear and offered it to a prostitute.

Perhaps he was schizophrenic or epileptic. In any case, as madness was drawing ever closer, he decided to have himself admitted to the Saint-Rémy hospital. There he worked relentlessly, painting over 150 pictures and making a hundred drawings or so. His meadows and cornfields are alive with

60 – Georges Seurat. *The Coast at Bas-Butin, Honfleur* (detail) – Musée des Beaux-Arts, Tournai.

wide undulations; olive trees with gnarled trunks join the cypresses that star his landscapes (*The Cypresses*, 1889, plate 58).

In May 1890 his brother Théo took him back to Paris but, as the noisy Paris life tired him, Vincent made up his mind to settle at Auvers, in Valmondois, where Doctor Gachet took charge of him, taught him etching and induced him to paint, as he was convinced that it constituted an excellent therapy. It was the beginning of a deep friendship. Van Gogh painted the wide landscape that spread in front of his eyes and the surrounding villages (*Thatched Cottages at Cordeville*, 1890, plate 55). He was delighted by the cornfields stretching along the plain which attracted flocks of ravens when it was time for the harvest.

A few days before his death he was to paint three such landscapes (*Crows in the Wheatfields*, Auvers, 1890, plate 59),

and they express all his solitude and sadness. On July 27th he shot himself through the heart with the very same pistol he had been lent to kill ravens; he died three days later attended by his brother Théo.

In 1886, the same year that Vincent van Gogh arrived in Paris and Gauguin went to Brittany for the first time, Impressionism split up and Neo-Impressionism was officially born. It was Signac who gave this name to the new trend, also known as Divisionism or Pointillism, a name which the Paris group strongly rejected.

In 1886 the Divisionists took part in the last impressionist exhibition to which they had been invited by Pissarro who showed his pictures along with theirs.

Georges Seurat (1859-1891) and Paul Signac (1863-1935) had met in 1884 at the Salon des Indépendants where artists who had been refused for the official Salon exhibited their

61 – Paul Signac. *The French Riviera* – 1889. Haags Collection, The Hague.

paintings; among those was Albert Dubois-Pillet (1846-1890), one of the promoters of the exhibition, who was to become famous in 1886.

When they began painting, Seurat and Signac clearly acknowledged their love for Impressionism, depicting the same themes, in Paris for Signac and along the coasts of Brest for Seurat.

Together they experimented with colour, restricting their chromatic composition to the four fundamental colours (blue, red, yellow and green) in their various tones. They rationalized the rendering of colour by using small colour dots which, by blending directly in the eye, created a more intense luminosity than that which was obtained by merely mixing colours on the palette or by superimposing brushstrokes on the surface of the canvas.

The two painters shared a common love for the sea: Seurat painted in Normandy and Brittany (*The Coast at Bas-Butin, Honfleur*, plate 60) and Signac on the Atlantic coast where he spent his summers.

He was the first to "discover" the French Riviera (*The French Riviera*, 1889, plate 61) and in 1893 bought a house at Saint-Tropez where he generously entertained all his friends. In the last years of their lives, all the Impressionists who had accepted living in misery for the sake of painting freely and had gone from one place to another in search of a spot that suited their needs, began to become famous, except Sisley, who went on living miserably.

They were thus able to live a little more comfortably. But the world they had immortalized was disappearing, and they all felt that they were mere survivors who left in their works in memory of a world they had cherished and from which they had drawn their inspiration.

Editor in chief Anna Maria Mascheroni

Art director Ettore Maiotti

Text Simonetta Venturi

Translation Pierre Remords

Production Art, Bologna

Photo credits Gruppo Editoriale Fabbri S.p.A., Milan

Copyright © 1989 by Gruppo Editoriale Fabbri S.p.A., Milan

Published by Park Lane
An Imprint of Grange Books Ltd
The Grange
Grange Yard
LONDON
SE1 3AG

ISBN 1-85627-239-7

This edition published 1993

Printed in Italy by Gruppo Editoriale Fabbri S.p.A., Milan